MW00636483

DAG Publishing
DAG World.com

First printing, 2021

ISBN 978-0-9995324-0-9

Design By Ronald Brown of Brown Digital Design

ACKNOWLEDGMENTS

WOW. Where do I begin? Over the past seven years, I have had countless conversation about Weak-Day Remedies, some good and some bad. Every person and every conversation played a vital role in helping me get this book out. Therefore, I publicly thank you all.

I would like to give a special acknowledgement to Joe Natal, my business partner, mentor and book coach. He gave life to my visions. Thank you, Joe.

First, all honor and praise go to God. It is because of Him, that I am. In Spite my faults, He continues to use me to restore others. I am eternally grateful.

Secondly, I truly thank my wife Tiffany and daughters, Brittney, Victoria and Davye. They have sacrificed much time with me while I birthed this book.

Finally, My Granny V. Essie Ransom and my mother Ruby A. Gethers. Words cannot begin to express how appreciative I am for all the prayers, sacrifices and love you two have given me. During those moments when I wanted to quit on life, you two were there. Mom, I can still hear your powerful words in my ear: you said, "if I don't give up on you, you would not give up on me, and together we would make it." How right you were! Ma, WE MADE IT.

INTRODUCTION

Weak-Day Remedies is David's medicine for life's pains, heartbreaks and disappointments.

A "Weak-Day" isn't something that just happens Monday – Friday. In a real sense a Weak-Day can happen any day: holiday, birthday, anniversary, an ordinary day or over the course of many days. A Weak-Day is when life has hit you so hard, you don't think you can face tomorrow, you are so overwhelmed, you can't see the light at the end of the tunnel, or when there is no fight left in you and you want to throw in the proverbial towel. This is how I felt during a 30-year prison sentence.

After being released from prison, earning two degrees in five years, starting two successful businesses, and speaking to thousands of people across the country, I am often asked how did I transform my life? Weak-Day Remedies is the answer to that question. I journaled my way to transformation.

I invite you on my journey of transformation and challenge you to a transformation of your own.

The journal entries found in Weak-Day Remedies are originals from my time in prison. They are raw, un-edited and un-censored to maximize your experience. In the beginning words are misspelled, my usage of the English vernacular is poor and sentencing structuring is horrible. However, as I matured and transformed, so did my writing skills.

As you read Weak-Day remedies and take the transformation challenge, I ask that you give yourself the grace to start where you are and then push yourself to transform into the best you, God created you to be. If I can do it, YOU CAN TOO.

TRANSFORMATION TOPICS

Jan. 11, 2004   5:42 P.M.   "Anger"

Being in prison makes it hard for me not to get angry. Especially, when I have had a bad day. My anger is one of the main reasons that I am in prison today. That is why it is important to me to do something about my anger. When I get mad, I literally what to hurt - be it metally or physically - the person(s) that has caused my anger. I want them to fill pain like they caused me anger.

Recently, I allowed this girl to get me mad. So mad that I wanted her to feel the full strength of my wrath. I wanted to say some things to her that I knew would hurt her mentally and for a long time. By us being friends, I knew exactly how to hurt her.

However, It was only by the grace of God that I did not do it. Even As I write this entry I am still mad at her. What caused my anger was her being lazy. But even worse than that is that I did not notice how close I had allowed us to become.

What I thought was a simple friend ship, proved to be more. Now, I am in a bad situation. Because of my anger toward her, I realize that I have deep feelings for this woman. What else would be the cause of such anger.

Before _____ came into my life, I was content on doing my time in prison alone. I realize that no one owes me nothing. So her coming into my life was refreshing. Well now that she is hear, I feel like she is playing game with me. Those feelings is whats causing me to become angry with her.

Lately, she has not been doing anything that she say she is going to do. When I question her about it, she tells me "that no matter what, she is always thinking about me." I find that hard to believe.

I would respect her more and not be angry with her if she was completely honest with me about our friendship. Her lies and dishonesty is a sign of disrespect towards me. I have been completely honest and a true friend to her and her actions towards me now makes me angry and want to hurt her.

But God is changing me everyday to not allow any one to still my Joy and Peace. I am going to try to work things out with _____ however, I cannot continue to allow her to hurt me. David Scott

1. ANGER

VI-XXVIII-IV 2:45 P.M. "Happiness"

For most of us happiness is based on artificial accoutrements, ie; money, job, house, spouse, kids or anything else that we allow to define who we are. As I approach my 32nd birthday I realize that I have spent a great portion of my life in search of the wrong kind of happiness. In a real sense how I feel about who I am and a solid relationship with God is my true happiness. I have been in prison almost six years and if it had not been for God's grace and mercy I don't know where I would be. Things that I thought made me happy (women, money, clothes + friends) have all failed me since I have been in prison. And now here I am left only with my mother, a few friends, a few family members and God. And believe it or not I am truly the happiest man alive. Don't get me wrong, there is alot of things that I would love to have (a relationship with my daughter, my freedom, a good woman) however, I have learned to live without them. For most of us it takes some major setback or difficulties for us to realize what are true happiness is. It is when we lose all that which we've placed our hope in that we are open to experience true happiness. I often tell people that prison is the best thing that has ever happen to me. It is through my time in prison that I discovered true happiness. Others find it through the death of a loved one, cancer, some other type of terminal sickness or loss. It is at that moment of our greatest sorrow that we see how insignificant our material things are. It is at that moment that we need something greater in order to make it. That something greater is God. In the midst of all the turmoil God gives us peace. The kind of peace that can't be taken away. Now that I have this inner peace it is my job not to allow anyone or anything to take my peace away. Getting this peace in my life was no easy task and keeping it is going to be even greater. I can now face any arduous situation knowing that God and my peace will get me through. I can live the rest of my life without the so called finer things in life because I have the real finer thing in life. That being God. I am no fool, I know there are going to be many more challenges in my life. However, I am better equipped to face and handle those challenges

_____

_____

_____

_____

_____

_____

_____

_____

_____

_____

_____

_____

_____

_____

_____

_____

X-IV-MMIV 10:45 A.M. "Desire + Prayer"

We all have certain desires and prayers. Some selfish and some pure. But regardless of what kind they are, they are ours. A man can often be driven according to his desires and prayers. If not pure, your desires and prayers can destroy you and the very life that you have or seek after.

When I was a young lad my only desire was women and sex. And the fulfillment of that desire led me to Kill a man, which sent me to prison.

Now, as a more maturer adult my heart's desire and prayer is that I may truly get to know God in a much better way. Afterall, what good is your desire and prayer if God does not first put it in your spirit.

When your desires and prayers are that of God not only will you reach and achieve those desires and prayers. But God will provide away for those desires and prayers.

In-order to reach my heart's desire and prayer I know I need to seek God. God has a plan for my life. Eventhough I might be enduring through some trails and tribulations, I know that these are the mere obstacles that God is using to help me navigate my way through life.

Also, it is through these same trails and tribulation that I find out what God's desire is for me.

Many of us fall short of our desires because they are too self-centered. We have the mentality of "I want this, that and the other". However, when we are walking in the desires of the Lord, all of the selfish accoutrements that we desire will be added unto us. But it is hard for us to put our desires on the back-burner for God's desires. By nature we our selfish people only thinking about ourselves.

Oh, but if we ever catch on to the real meaning of the scripture that says, "Seek ye first the Kingdom of God and His righteousness and all these things will be added unto you", what a heart-filled desired life would we live.

Your desire should always began with and end with God. For it is He who has redeemed us for His desire and His desire only.

3. DESIRE AND PRAYER

_____
_____
_____
_____
_____
_____
_____
_____
_____
_____
_____
_____
_____
_____
_____
_____
_____

April 24, 2005 "My Desire"

My true desire today is to move into another realm in my relationship with God. I do not want to be one with a form of Godliness. Nor do I want to be someone who read and use the bible as a cliche.

Rather, I chose to be an individual who's life, ways and footsteps are ordered and guided by the will and Word of God. I want God's Spirit to dwell in me, I want God's Spirit to live in me. I want God's spirit to encompass me round about.

I have played games long enough. It is time that I be either hot or cold – I chose hot. Luke warm God spits out His mouth. I want my life to begin to bear the fruit of God and His righteous in my life. I want my life to change the lives of those around me. Starting with my family and friends.

In-order for this to happen it starts with a commitment from me to read, pray and touch bases with God daily. Nothing can become more important than that. I must hunger and thirst after His spirit, word and righteousness.

I must show a true desire to want to be filled with the Holy Spirit. As I do this God will be faithful and just to fill me with His spirit and I will begin to fill His pressence in my life.

The more God dwells in me, the more I become like Him. After all, I am made in His image and likeness. Everyday is a chance to become more like Him.

I must also commit to having my mind renewed daily by the word of God. I have to believe the words that I read and begin to apply them to my daily living.

Finally, there can be no laziness. Regardless of how tired I may feel. I must do what it takes in-order to spend time with God.

Heaven is my goal. I am just a pilgram on earth. Therefore, my actions and life must reflect that of one going to heaven. I can't let the trival things of life cause me to lose focus.

Being the man God has called me to be is a reality that I now accept and as of today, no-more living below that which I was created to be.

Dear God please accept me today. Allow your spirit and pressence to dwell in me. Forgive me for being less than the man you called me to be. I love you God and present my body to you as a living sacrifice you use as you please Amen. David a. Setthew.

4. MY DESIRE

Jan. 11, 2009 "Never Give Up"

There is nothing that we can get into, or go through that God can't bring us out of or through. God arms are not short that they cannot save. His ears always hears. His eyes always sees.

Beloved, no one ever told you that the road would be easy. And God has not brought you this far to leave you. As you read, study, mediatate and learn God's Word. You will find out that your story is already written. God is the author and finisher of your faith.

According to the Word of God we win every battle that we face. Yes, we must go through heart ache and pain, but we win. We must go through sickness and death, but we win. We must go divorces and losses, but we win. No weapon formed against shall prosper. God never said that we wouldn't have things come against us. However, everything that comes against us is working for our good.

The bible say in the end we shall come forth as pure Gold. And like gold we must go through a refining process. The refining process is to remove doss from the gold. Doss is the imperfections and impurities and we need to rid our selve of the sins + weight that so easily make us fall away from God.

So no matter what you may be faced with giving up is not an option. Because God is on our side we don't have to throw in the towel. Nor do we have to wave the white flag of surrender.

God knows what you are going through. And He will not put more on you than you can bear. In the midst of what you are facing and going through, trust God. His ways are perfect, His Word is proven, true and trustworthy. And He is a shield, buckler and protector of them that trust Him.

Read God's Word for yourselve and found out that you are a' overcomer. Find out that you are the head and not the tail. Find out that you are above and not beneath.

You never have to give up on life, love or hope. You never have to give up on your dreams and goals. But more importantly, you don't have to give up on God.

Ask God for the strength to go on. I don't feel no ways tired. I come to far from where I started from...

David a. Brothers

Decisions

Jan. 17, 2009 "Wheat + Tares", "Good + Evil".

Has there ever been a time where you had to make a very important decision. A decision that was between good + evil, Right + wrong. And making the correct decision isn't as easy as one would think.

I would even take it a step further d\u2026 say that you are trying to make a decision between two things that are right.

Today, I am caught trying to decide between two women. Neither is a bad choice. However, only one is the right choice. So how I do I make the right decision?

I've decided that I wouldn't rush to make a choice. And regardless of how much pressure I am under, continue to take my time. I hear your thoughts afar off. You're saying that isn't fair to the two women. And you're right. However, I am not sleeping with neither nor am I in a relationship with either.

I am very much aware that both women would like to be apart of my permanently. Nevertheless, I am not in position to make a sound decision. Furthermore, there are too many unaccountable varible that must be taken into consideration.

So the most important thing for me to do is be very honest with all parties involved, so that they may do what is best for them. Afterall, their free to make a decision that best suits them or benefits thems. Because I never want to have some one's life hanging in the balance of my un-decesion.

Then there is prayer. Seeking God's face has always proven to be the best choice. Allowing God to reveal which one is best suited for my life style in Him is key. I would hate to be with the one that pleases me physically but not spiritually and vice versa.

The whole man must be completely satisfied. Because when we're not it leads to trouble And trouble is something that I can't afford.

So I am going to allow the wheat and tares grow together and let God do the separating. Only He can seperate the two and show me which one is best for me.

Dala Settles

6. DECISIONS

_____

_____

_____

_____

_____

_____

_____

_____

_____

_____

_____

_____

_____

_____

_____

_____

_____

Feb 3, 2009 "It Is Not About Me"

I am learning a very powerful lesson during my years in prison. It is a painful and very difficult lesson. However, is has proven to be a very beneficial lesson. And that lesson is "That it isn't all about me."

My life is no longer my life. My life has been brought with a price. That price is the blood of Jesus. The purchaser is God Himself.

While I was yet a sinner Jesus died for me that I might inherit the Kingdom of heaven and salvation. While I was living my life in a way that was pleasing to me. Selling drugs. Using and abusing alcohol. Using and abusing women. Lieing, stealing, deceiving and taking advantage of people. Committing adultery and fornication. Not being a father to my beautiful daughter. You name it. Inspite my doing all of that Christ died for me.

He didn't wait until I confessed to Him. He didn't wait until I started to believing in Him. He didn't wait until I called on His name. He didn't wait until I became saved and a member of His family. No He did it while I was still stuck in the hands of sin.

What a great example of love. Unconditional love. Especially, in a day and time when we do everything based on motives. God's only motive was love. He says in His Word that

God so loved the world that He gaves His only begotten Son.

The only thing that God wants in return is that we live our lives for Him. That we become willing vessels. When we begin to really see what has been done on our behalf it becomes life changing.

Jesus died for me. That has become personal. I can't help but to start living for Him. It is not about David A. Geffers anymore. It is all about Jesus Christ and Him cruxified. It is about living my life the way God intended for me to live it.

In order for me to do that, I must present myself to God daily as a living sacrifice, Holy and acceptable to Him. I must deny myself, take up my cross and follow Him. There is a way that seems right to man, but it's paths lead to death. God's paths lead to Godliness and righteousness.

God, I turn my life over to you, that you may use it as you please. That you may use me to further the agenda of heaven. Use me Lord to model Christ before others that they might be saved. It is not about me anymore God. But it is all about you. *David a Keith*

_____

_____

_____

_____

_____

_____

_____

_____

_____

_____

_____

_____

_____

_____

_____

_____

_____

Feb. 8, 2009 "Chasing My Goals"

God has given me a vision. A vision that has been written on the tablet of my heart. It is a vision that I whole heartedly accepts. My desire is to fulfill this vision to the best of my natural abilities, as well as with the help of God.

To accomplish this goal I must first seek God as to what to do, which way to go and how am I to get it done. The bible says seek yea first the Kingdom of God and His righteousness and He will direct they path.

As I seek God with my whole heart I am given instruction on how to fulfill the vision that He has given me. The vision has been placed in my heart by God, So I will be a fool not to seek Him.

Also, I must lay aside every sin and weight that easily ensares me. That means anything that causes me to stuble and fall short of God's glory & vision.

Just recently, a show came on T.V - "For the Love of Ray J". Man, this show had everyone in an uproar. There were women barely dressed on TV, doing all type of sexually things to please, Ray J. Yes, I watched, but then realized that watching this program is causing me to stumble.

I truly want to live for God and be the man He called me to be. Living day by day for God has become a priority. I can't allow the lust of the flesh or the pride of life to cause me to miss the mark.

For me, it was easy for me to miss the mark. It was easy for me to give in to the lust of the flesh. But no more.

How can I call myself a child of God yet give in to every temptation of sin. that comes my way. Being truly committed to God in action is a must.

I am looking forward to seeing the power of God in my life. And I know that the more unrighteous things that I give up and lay aside the more God is going to do and give me. No good things will He withhold from me if I walk upright before Him. And walking up right before God isn't a hard thing to do. The only requirement is that you have a desire to do so.

I have that desire. I am determined to have what God has for me. My goals are too important to let them slip away because of sin. Chasing my goals is my priority. And I can only do it through God.

David A. Stitt

March 7, 2009 "Sowing & Reaping"

The philosophy of Sowing & reaping is one of common practice. We sow during the appriate seasons and we reap during the appriate seasons. The practice is so common that it has become second nature to us. But do we know just what it is that we practice? Do we truly understand what sowing and reaping is?

Sowing has many meanings to convey it's point. But one that I like is: to extend. That mean to prolong; make larger; to give; to grant. When you read scriptures from that definitions viewpoint it hits home.

Gal. 6:7 "Whatever a man sows- Whatever he prolongs. Whatever he makes larger. Whatever he gives or grants...

What are you sowing? Is it the righteousness of God. Is it His Peace. Is it His love. Is it His Compassion, grace & mercy. Or are you sowing the things of the flesh, ie. Lust, selfishness, greed, hatred, discord.

The unique thing about sowing is that it is an intentional act. A deliberate act. A willfull and knowing act on our behalf. With a conscious mind we extend that which our hearts desires. We do not accedentally sow love or hate we do either consciously. We don't accidentally sow good or bad we do either consciously.

However, while we are out on our journey of sowing, we forget that there will be an harvest. There will be reaping.

What is harvesting? I like this definition; the outcome of any effort. Back to our Scripture ... that shall he reap. That shall be the outcome of any of his efforts. In a real sense man takes in the results of his intentionally deeds.

With that being Sowing + Reaping clearly being defined. What are you intentionally sowing? Think about it. Because you will surely harvest the efforts that you sow.

Also, keep in mind how you sow. If you sow sparingly. You will harvest sparingly. If you sow cheerfully, you will reap cheerfully.

Your process of sowing and reaping should be one of great thought and consideration. Stop sowing haphazardly. Sow as God will your heart to sow. Sow as you would like to harvest.

Dear God, My heart's desire is to be the sower that you have called me to be. I want to move larger and extend and give that which you give me to give. Have your way in Jesus' name.

David A. Betters

_____

_____

_____

_____

_____

_____

_____

_____

_____

_____

_____

_____

_____

_____

_____

_____

_____

March, 11, 2009 "Wilderness Experience" EX 13. 17-18

All of us at one particular time or another will find ourselves in a wilderness. A place where we just let go our past. And we waiting to go into our future. We've just come out of a situation that was bad for us and were awaiting instructions on what to do next. In a real sense, our wilderness is sort of a place of limbo. We can't go back-wards, however, we're not ready to move forward. We're literally stuck in the middle.

Now some people may look at this as a bad things. Some may even blame you and call you indecisive because your in limbo. Others still may say that you're afraid to make a move.

But I a here to tell you that all of that is not true. Limbo is not a bad place to be. In the wilderness is not a bad place to be. Especially, if limbo and the wilder-ness that you're in you were led their by God.

I have found myself in many situations where I wasn't led by God. And the hell and turmoil that accompanied that sit-uation wasn't good. But our Godly wilder-ness experiences have great benefits if you allow God to deal with you as He see fits.

I hear the voice of critics loud and clear

in my ear," How can being in the wilderness be a good experience."

First, being in the wilderness gives you a chance to stand still. The worse thing for any of us to do is move premature or too quickly.

Second, being in the wildness allows you the opportunity to see the salvation of God. Our eyes have the tendecy to decive us, so we want to see what God see.

Third, being in the wilderness allow us to listen to the voice of God. We hear alot of things and get counsel from many areas. But the counsel of God is the best.

Before you come out of your wilderness experience make sure you Stop. Look. And Listen. God led you into the wilderness so that He may instruct and prepare you for your promise land. God will not let you go into your promise land unprepared.

If you find yourself in the wilderness think it not strange. Yield yourself to God and allow Him to shape, form and mold you for your promise land. There is a promise land for you following with milk + honey. Recieve it today.

Dawida Mathews

_____

_____

_____

_____

_____

_____

_____

_____

_____

_____

_____

_____

_____

_____

_____

_____

_____

March 15, 2009 "Seeing The Hand of God..." I Kings 17

Truth be told we're all looking for something. We're looking love, peace, acceptance. We're looking comfort, friendships, stability. We're looking for anything that would make our present situation different from what it is now. We're looking for away out or in. We're looking for away up or down. We spend a great deal of our lives looking, looking looking.

Some of us are fortunate to find what we are looking and searching for. The rest are not so fortunate. Those who do find only keep what they have found temporary before they are back in the rat race of life tring to find something that brings only temporary satisfaction to a situation.

I am reminded of the book "Who moved my Cheesed", were they were 4 mice: Hem, Haw, Scurry + Sniff. Every morning they would get up early in the morning looking for cheese. They always found cheese at cheese station "A". Until one morning they went to cheese station "A" and to their shocking amazement cheese station "A" no longer had cheese.

The success, fame, love, peace, comfort, stability and e.t.c. that they had found at cheese station "A" was only temporary. And so hear they were out searching and looking once again.

I said all of that just to say this. That

44

in order to find that which brings total peace + stability to our lives. Can only be found in God.

When Elijah listen to the voices of God and when Elijah did what God had commanded him to. He begin to see the hand of God active in his life. We miss the hand of God and the provision of God and the providence of God because our eyes and attention is focused on things that bring only temporary satisfaction.

As long as we are focused on the wrong things we will continue to find Cheese Station "A" barren and bare. But when we put all our attention and focus and faith in and on God we will find complete and total peace, love and comfort.

For in God can be found the essential things needed for the substantiation of life here on earth and in eternity. Our search has not to be in vain anymore.

Seek the Lord while He may be found... Look to the hills, from which comes all your help... He that hunger and thirst after righteousness shall be filled. Place your mind intentionally on those things which are above. God wants to give you eternal peace, love and comfort.

David A. Gethers

March 26, 2009 "Trouble Free" John 14:1

Trouble, Trouble, Trouble. Here some trouble, there some trouble everywhere some trouble. Man born of woman is a few days and full of trouble. And despite us living in a state of incessant trouble, Jesus tells us not to let our hearts be troubled.

What is trouble? Trouble is to distrub or agitate; to worry + harass; to cause inconvenience, to take pains; a state of mental distress; worry.

Jesus is asking us to not let our hearts worry. Not to let us become distress and agitated by life's uncertain situations that may or may not occur.

We worry because we have a lack of faith in the outcome of a given situation. We're not sure if things are going to turn out the way we hope or want.

In Mark 6:45 Jesus told the diciples to get into the boat and go before Him to the otherside. Now you would think that the diciple wouldn't have anything to worry about. You would think that they had no reason for their hearts to be troubled. Afterall, It was Jesus Himself, who said let us go to the other side.

The outcome of their trip was guranteed. Regardless of what situations came up and regardless of what difficulties you may face, they were promised by Jesus to make it to the otherside.

We have a promise from God that He would never leave you nor forsake you. So when life's difficulties come upon you let not your heart be troubled. When money problems arise let not your heart be troubled. When family problems come up let not your heart be troubled. When you're trying to raise children by yourself, let not your heart be troubled.

By no means will anything that you face harm you or destroy you. Therefore let not your heart be troubled. If you believe in Jesus, believe what He has said about you. God is not slack concerning His promise towards you. Yeah, the promise might not manifest it imediatly but with God it shall come to pass.

My heart is free from trouble because I am persuaded in Him whom I believe that He is able to keep me until that day. My life is in God's hands.

I am free praise the Lord I am free No longer bond no more changes holding me It just a blessing.

Davita Gethers

49

July 7, 2009 "Overcoming" Col. 3:1-11

At some point in all of our lives we are faced with something that we must over-come. Be it addictions. Such as sexual, drugs gambling or alcohol. We also have to over-come situations, problem, people, places and things. Try as we might, we all are overtaken by a fault. Some things just gets the best of us. And for awhile we are taken under by whatever it is.

But God's people are more than conqueurs we are overcomers. With the right Biblical tools we can overcome any situation that we face.

In Colossians 3, verse 2 it says "Set Your Mind". When you are trying to be-come an overcomer you must intentionally deleberately, willfully and knowingly place your mind higher than what it is use to. You can no longer think like an addict and overcome. You can't think like a failure and overcome. You can't think like a quitter and overcome. You can't think like a loser and over come. You can't think and have negative thoughts and expect to over come.

James Allen says In his book "As You Think" and I quote " The Key to our personal power is in our minds." We must re-program our minds to think like an overcomer. What we feed the mind to eat is how it will grow and think.

Colossian 3 teaches us to think on those things that are above. Think on those things that are right.

In Philippian we are told to think on that what ever things are noble, just, pure, lovely and of good report. Also, in Philippian we are taught to have the same mind that was in Christ Jesus.

In Roman 12:2 we are taught to be transformed by the renewing of our minds. That means shifting our mindset from that of death to life. From wrong to right. From negative to positive.

We are the head and not the tail. We are above and not beneath. We are first and not last. We are the lenders and not the borrowers. We have got to start seeing ourselves as God intend for us to be. Our family + friends do not determine who we are.

A lowly mindset will cause us to act and behave in a low life state. And a Godly mindset will cause us to act and behave as the kings and Queens God created us to be. David a. Dethers.

13. OVERCOMING

2 Sam. 5:1-10

July 12, 2009 " Stronghold & Addictions "

Strongholds and addictions are the same words on the same coin, just on different sides. Spiritually, we call it a stronghold. Medically, it is called an addiction. Nevertheless, no matter what you call it, if we are overtaken by it, we must face it and deal with it.

We can not allow it to linger in our lives. The longer that we allow it to hang around the stronger it becomes. The stronger it becomes the less control we have over it. When we no longer have control it becomes a stronghold or addiction.

Whenever a stronghold or addiction exist in our lives we are incomplete. And most addictions and strongholds spring forth because of a lack in our lives. We didn't have this that or the other growing up so our stronghold or addiction makes up for that lack.

Most if not all of our addictions and strongholds can be traced back to some part of our childhood or a traumatic experience that we may have had in our life. And when anything associated with our childhood or traumatic experience rises it's ugly head if we are not strong in the Lord we begin to engage in destructive behavior to cope with that which we don't want to deal with.

However, strongholds and addictions don't have any power over us. For the bible says in LK 10:19 "That Jesus has given us power over all the power of the enemy, and nothing shall by any means hurt us".

David, realized that the stronghold in his life was blind, lame, weak and powerless. And when he realized that, he was able to break the hold that the stronghold had on and over him.

Whatever stronghold or addiction that may be in your life is blind, lame, weak and powerless. It doesn't have power or control over you. You can defeat it by the power of God that is in you. Greater is He that is in you... That He, that is in you, is God, Jesus and The Holy Spirit.

Starting today, starting right now exercise your power over any strongholds or addictions. You can't, nor will you ever be whole and complete unless you eliminate all the strongholds and addictions in your life.

God wants to make you whole in Him. Will you let Him.

David A. Dethers

_____

_____

_____

_____

_____

_____

_____

_____

_____

_____

_____

_____

_____

_____

_____

_____

_____

Psalm 103:2

July 17, 2009 "Don't Forget What God has Done"

God is truly Good. God has been good to us. God will be good to us. This is something that is easily forgotten when the vicissitudes of life begin to get the best of us.

Let your spouse make you mad about something. Do you respond "you always do that". When the truth of the matter is, this is the first time, but because you are mad you forget all the good that has been done.

When your children come home late from being out, or get one or two bad grades on their report card. Do you say "you're always messing up"?

When you lose your job, can't pay your bills, get past due notices in the mail and to make a hellish situation all the more hellified you just got sick and don't have any insurance. Do you say, "Bad things always happen to me?"

Why do we always take a victims mind set and attitude when things don't go our way. More importantly, who ever said that everything would always go our way? Who ever said that it would be all sunshine and no rain? Why do we want the good of God but don't want the bad.

Job said "Man born of a woman is a

few days and full of trouble. Arduous times befalls all of us. And when they do, it is important that we have a very good memory. We must remember all the good days that God has given us and shown us. We must remember the good times and all the benefits of God.

I am not saying that what you are go through right now isn't difficult. I am not being insensitive to your present plight. Nor am I suggesting that you ignore or push to the side the unpleasent moments that you face or are facing.

However, what I am saying is to think about what God has done for you. Philippians 4:8-Says" Whatever things are true, noble, just, pure, lovely, good and praise worthy to think and meditate on these things. The more we think about the goodness of God, the better we will feel.

Today, place your mind, intentionally, willfully and deliberately think about all the good that you have experienced over the years all at the hands of God. Rejoice over all the benefits that He has bestowed on you. David a Botts

application / Remedy

July 22, 2009 "How to Please God" Heb. 11:6

Faith is the best and easiest way to please God. Without faith it is impossible to please God. Exercising our faith pleases God. Exercise means- An act of Employing or putting into play ; use.

Faith is like instant Kool-Aid, Instant Kool-Aid Contains everything it needs. It has the flavor and sugar in it already. All you have to do is add/Mix water and you produce what you want.

In a real sense when you add/Mix action to your faith. It pleases God, thus Causing Him to produce that which your heart desires or that which He has ordained for you.

It isn't our job to understand the intricate and enigmatic details of God's plan for our lives. And even if was to share and show us the Complete plan for our lives (Gen. 18:17). It would still be an ambigious maze that we couldn't figure out.

Because His thoughts are not our thoughts. His ways are not our ways. His are much higher and advanced then we Can imagine or think. That which we are able to ask and

fathom is minute in the grand Know
ledge and wisdom of God.
   There fore, if you really want to please
God, walk by faith and not by sight.
You might can't see that child life
or even your life turning around. But
have faith that it will. You might not
be able to see the job that God has
for you. But have faith that there is
a job. You might not be to see how
you can live life with out this person
or that person. But have faith the you
can. You might not be able to see how
God is going to restore that marriage
and family. But have faith that He will.
You might not be able to see how
all of this is going to work out for
your good. But have faith that it will.
You might not be able to see how
God is going to heal you and deliver
you. But have faith that He will.
   Faith without action is dead. Mix
action with your faith. Please God
today. Walk and have faith.
   When a man ways pleases God,
He will give him the desires of his
heart. David A. Gethers.

July 28, 2009 "Do You Know Who You Are?"

Insecurity is a plague that affect many belivers. Beautiful people are stricken, with insecurity. Rich people are stricken by insecurity. Famous people are stricken by insecurity, as well.

Insecurity isn't a poor man's, un-at tractive or less fortunate man's plague. Neither is insecurity bound by race ethnicity or religous beliefs. Insecurity is an equal oppurtunity plague that threaten, harass and attacks anyone who do not know who they are in Christ Jesus.

Society does not have the right to call you beautiful or unattractive, rich or poor a have or have not. In fact, society nor circumstances have a right to determine who you are. Your identity is pre-determined by God alone. Your are Choosen by God alone (1 Chron. 29:1).

We are told in Gen. 1:26 that you are made in God's image and likeness. Duet. 28:12-13, says "That you are the lender not the borrower, You're the head and not the tail, You are above and not be- neath. 1 Pet. 1:3-5, states" that you have been called to a living hope and that you have an inheritance that can't fade away. Nor can society take it away

From you. It is reserved for you in heaven. 1 Pet. 2:9, Calls you a royal priesthood, a chosen generation, a holy nation. His own special people. Who was once not His people, but now you are. You once had no mercy but now have mercy. You were once lost by now you are found. Rev. 1:56, identifies you as Kings and Priests of God.

We must start seeing, believing and Knowing who we are according to the Word of God. We can't allow outside circumstances and situations detect dictate who we are in God. We are the Elect of God. The devil would lead us to believe that we are everything but a Child of God. But he is a liar. He is defeated. You are a Conqueror. You can do and have whatever God has said is yours. You don't have to second guess God.

Take God at His Word. Live Victorious Kill and eliminate any insecurities that would cause you to miss out on the Best that God has for you.

David A. Dethero
Remedy

_____

_____

_____

_____

_____

_____

_____

_____

_____

_____

_____

_____

_____

_____

_____

_____

_____

Aug. 7, 2009 "Apple of God's Eye" Pro. 7:2, Deut. 32:10

God sees us His people, His Choosen ones those whom He has Called, ordainded and set apart - as the apple of His eye.

The object of His affection and love. Some one that He tenderly loves and care about. Someone that He Commune with and talks to. Someone that He protects Covers and goes out of His way for. Some-one that He provides for. Someone that He would sacrifice His only son for.

God, thinks very highly of you and I. So much so that while we were yet sinners that He gaves us His only begotten son.

God Cared so much for the Children of Israel that when they were in bondage back in Egypt, He sent Moses to deliver them out of the hands of Phorhoh. And after that, God proved His love for them again by parting the red sea and giving them a way of escape from an angry mob that was hot and fast on thier tracks.

He went even further and while they were in the wilderness Complaining about the living Conditions, he gave them clothes that didn't tare up, shoes that didn't wear out and He gave them water from the Rock of Christ, manna from Heaven both day and night. But more importantly, He led them into their promise land. A land flowing with milk and honey. A land they didn't work for, nor did they til the ground. But yet He gave them a plentiful harvest.

He didn't do this because they were faithful. They worshipped all kinds of farience gods in the wilderness and in the promise land. He didn't do it because they had overwhelming faith. Because they didn't. They murmured and complained both in the wilderness and in the promise land. So much so that they wanted to return to Egypt instead of allowing God to lead them. He didn't do it because they were so good and kind. Because after all He had done for them, they became an abomination to Him.

God does what He does for us because we are the apple of His eye. We are His creation. We are made in His image and in His likeness. He wants us to experience His very best.

We have to begin to see and treat God as the apple of our eye. And His love and favor for us will overtake us.

Remedy   David A. Bethea

_____

_____

_____

_____

_____

_____

_____

_____

_____

_____

_____

_____

_____

_____

_____

_____

_____

_____

Pro. 25:24

Aug. 26, 2009 "Removing Contention"

Contention is strife or disputing. Arguing with another about a situation. Contention occurs most when we try to force our will upon others. Contention occurs when we feel that we have been wronged or disrespected. Contention occurs when we feel that we are always right and there is no room for someone else to inform or teach us that which we don't know.

Who wants to live in a state of incessant arguing and strife? Who wants to be in a relationship where there is constant nagging and bickering?

When a man has a contentious wife, lover, girlfriend or baby momma he has his hands full of trouble. When the woman that you are intimate with isn't happy, there is no happiness in that home. Contention removes the love joy, peace and stability of that home.

Us as men may think that the issue is of no importants or a minor issue that can be solved by a kiss gifts or a "I Love You". But to that woman she has become unsettled in her spirit. Thus, causing her to nag and bicker until she is content with the outcome.

At times we undervalue the importance of our wives being happy. Man lays the foundation for the house to be built upon. However, the woman, the wise woman builds her house. We must listen to our wives because she is our help meet. And God has given her sound wisdom that helps us and guide us.

Our wives are gifts from God. They are good and perfect gifts. Our wives add value to our lives and not sorrow. We obtain favor from God when we are married to a spirit filled woman of God. As the husband we must do all we can to remove any contention that may exist between us and our good thang. We don't need the balance in our homes to be off center because of a contentious wife. Her peace allows us the freedom we desire to do the things we want to do.

Remove contention from your marriage today. Don't allow the enemy to have place in your happy home.

Remedy

DaDa Sethus

_____

_____

_____

_____

_____

_____

_____

_____

_____

_____

_____

_____

_____

_____

_____

_____

_____

_____

_____

Psalm 37:4

Sept. 18, 2009 "Delight thyself in the Lord"

What does it really mean to delight thy self in the Lord. The Greek word for delight is "Anag" which means to be soft or pliable. To be easily bent; flexible. Easily influenced or persuaded. Adaptable. So what I saying?

In a real sense how much of your life is soft and pliable. When you make plans are the etched in stone? Or are they soft tentative plans that are at God's discretions. The bible says that man plans his ways but God has the final say so.

Do you think that you know better than God on how to lead your life? Do you feel that you know more than God about your life? When we go it alone without God's help we often find ourselves in a world of trouble. But that what life is like when we do not delight ourselves in the Lord.

God want people who are flexible, easily influenced by Him and not others. Someone that can be persuaded to do what is right and not wrong. God wants someone is adaptable, who can live there lives the way God wants them to live it.

When we delight in God we relinquish

our will for God's will. We abandon our
ways for God's ways. We seek counsel
of God and not ourselves.

When we delight in God we show Him
how much we need Him. How much we
love Him. How much we depend on Him
for our every need. God wants to see
if we really trust Him enough to say
not our will but thy will be done.

Jesus delighted Himself in doing the
will of God. He didn't think of Himself nor
what horrific death He would suffer on
our be halves. He took pleasure in
allowing Himself to be used by God.

God wants the same from us. He
created us and not we ourselfs. He created
us for a purpose. And when we do not
delight in Him He is unable to use
us effectively.

When we delight in the Lord we
are rewarded with the desires of our
heart. Those intimate secret things that
we really desire and want. God wants
to give you the abundant life. He wants
you to enjoy His goodness in the land
of the living. But we first must delight
completely in Him. Whole heartedly.

Darla Goss

Sept. 23, 2009 "God Responds To Our Words" Dan 10:12

There is this old saying" When E.F. Hutton speaks people listen." Well I would like to change that, when we speak God does all the listening. God looks and wait for His people to pray His words to Him.

Daniel was on his knees praying to God when the Angel of the Lord appeared to him and told him "that from the first time that he sat his heart and mind to understand and humble yourself *Himself* before God, that his words were heard by God". And that God had sent him to respond and act on His behalf because of thy words.

God responds to His words. Repeat God's words to Him in prayer and watch Him perform according to His word. However, we cannot speak God's word if we don't know God's word. We can't know God's word if we don't study, meditate and read God's word. We can't study, meditate and read God's word if we don't pick up God's word.

Most of us have these big, fancy, pretty bibles in our homes, but we use them for decorative ornaments in our homes. Our bible sit there years on in not even being touched for routine cleaning. But we wonder why God does not answer our prayers Because we know for sure that God "hears" the prayers of all. But only respond to the prayers of the right ous.

John says that we have not because we ask not. But Because we can't ask for what we don't know we are suppose to have. James says when we ask we ask amiss. We ask the wrong way and for the wrong things for all the wrong reasons.

Jesus tells us to ask anything in Jesus' name and it will be done so that the Father may be glorified in the son. We negate God's active power in our lives because we fail to understand and realize the Continual Connection that we have with Jesus Christ.

Jesus tells us that He would never leave us nor forsake us. And even when we are faithless He remains faithful. And God is not slack concerning His promises.

Give God a Chance to respond to your words. Whatever situation you have going on in your life, pray and talk to God about it. Have a little talk with Jesus tell Him all about your problem. He will make all things right. Dale Bell

_____

_____

_____

_____

_____

_____

_____

_____

_____

_____

_____

_____

_____

_____

_____

_____

_____

_____

Oct 21, 2009 Ps. 113 - 120 "Made up Mind"

The worse thing for anyone to be is double-minded. A person who can't make up their mind about what they want to do. Someone that waddle side to side over a decesion that needs to be made. (insert)

When we decide to believe in God and allow Him to be the head of our life that decision should be our final decision. The viscissitudes of life shouldn't cause us to go back on our decision to trust and follow God. Our love for God and His Word should be the anchor that keep us grounded in the word of God.

There is no need for us to return to our old ways. Why be like a dog returning to his vomit. Our old life and ways is what caused us to become sick in the first place. And because that life life style made us deathly sick we turned our life over to God. Now we must use the Word of God as our lamp for our feet and a light to our path.

Affliction is going to come our way. Trails and tribulations are going to come our way. Death, sickness and problems are sure to come. But the word of God will revive us. It will strengthen us. It will substain us. It will be our lifeline in the times of troubles.

During the time of trouble I find refuge in the word of God. The Word of God gives me hope. Keeping Gods Commandments is delightful.

We must be persuade in what we believe. Now that we are engrafted into Christ that is where we must stay. Our mind is made up. For God we have choose to live and for God we must die.

Paul decided to serve God with his whole life. Prison, beating, shipwreck, death threat and abandonment yet Paul held firm to his belief. jesus was betrayed, beatng and crucified. Yet He held on to His belief. David was anoitted to be King at a young age and endure persecution for the next 12 before coming King. But he also held on to his belief.

There should be no turning back from this point on. We have a cloud of witnesses who endured hardship and trails without giving up faith and trust in God.

No one said that the road would be easy, but we have the word of God to make the road bearable.

David A. Betts

God's Plan, Purpose + Promise
Eph. 1:11

June 27, 2010

There is an inheritance that every Child of God has coming to him. That inheritance is predestined according to the purpose of God. And God is working all things out for you according to the Counsel -deliberate determination- of His will - Heart's desire.

As human it is hard to see just what God has planned for us. And to make matters worse. We have a tendency to put our two cents in the planning.

God knows the plans concerning every man dwelling on the face of the earth and God has appointed our times and boundaries. But more importantly they are preset plans and even if God showed us the blue print of our lives we still wouldn't understand what we saw.

For the thoughts of God are much more advanced than our thoughts. His are much higher than ours. God's thoughts come from a pure place towards us.

God has an expected end for us. And that end is good and not evil. That end is for us to prosper and not fail.

God loves us so much that He will reveal His plan for our lives to us. And it is up to us to submit to the will of God for our lives. When we do, He gives us the strength to do what He has ordained for us to do.

La Va. Bitther

Proverb 4:13

July 4, 2010

The word of God is our key to life.
As we follow and adhere to what God
says to us our lives become rich in
meaning. We must grab hold of the
word of God, and hold on to it tightly.
Letting go of God instructions is not
a option. We must guard the instructions of God with our life.

Do you ever wonder way certain
things in life don't seem to go your
way? Your prayers seem to go un-
answered. Murphy's law is always in
effect over your life. Bad luck is the
only luck you have. And bad breaks
is all that you experience.

We should first examine how have
we handled the instructions of God.
The bible commands that we acknowledge God in all our ways and
He shall direct our paths. Can you

honestly say that you acknowledged
God before you got in the midst of
the situation that you are presently
in?

Did you follow the instructions
that God gave you after you consult-
ed Him?

Most time when we acknowledge
God we don't follow His commands
Completely. Partial obedience to God's
word isn't obedience. And our obedience must come from heart.

Wheater our lives are good or
bad it is in direct proportion to
our handling of God's-words and
instructions.

When I following them life is good-
not trouble free. And when I don't, I
am praying & wishing that I had've
followed them. D.Ja. Hoos

Jan 24, 2011

The Integrity of My Christianity: Ps. 24:4

How truthful am I to what I
confess to be? You know that a
lawyer is who he say he his by
his practice. Therefore, you should
know a Christian by his practice.

As a Christian my entire life
should be one of integrity. My attitude
should have integrity. My behavior
should have integrity. My character
should have integrity. My decisions
should have integrity.

When other's look upon me they
should see a man of integrity. But
more importantly, when I am alone
and God is looking upon me He
should see a man of integrity. We
often walk in integrity to please
others who all they can do is talk
about us. Forgetting to walk in

integrity before the Savior who makes the decision rather we spend eternity in heaven or hell.

Living an dishonest life no longer sits well with my soul. I am convicted at the slightless form of dishonesty in my life. The bible says "That God looks to show favor on those who heart is loyal to Him."

Honesty is a principle that God holds in high esteem, and so should we. It shouldn't be so easy for us to walk in dishonesty. The integrity of our Christianity should always be on display.

Consciously think about the integrity of your Christianity when you're having conversations, watching T.V., with your friends, at work or etc. Think about it when your alone. David A. Mathis

_____
_____
_____
_____
_____
_____
_____
_____
_____
_____
_____
_____
_____
_____
_____
_____
_____
_____

"The Importance Of Time"

What are you doing with your time? How important is your time? To answer these questions and more about your time look at your life in relationship to time.

For me, I have to divide my time amoang many things. Therefore, it is important that I prioritize who or what gets my time first.

God is my first priority. That is proven by my actions. When I first get up I pray read some- thing that relates to God's word then meditate about what I read as I prepare for the day.

Everything I need to survive for the day can be found in the presence of God. In fact, the bible says" That the times of refreshing...

Come from the presence of the Lord." That refreshing and that time makes life peaceful to live. It doesn't eliminate my problems, however, it gives me comfort during my problems.

It has become easy to turn away from the vanities of this world to God. Because the temporary things of this world pales in comparrison to the richness of God. God's peace is permanate. God's love is permanate. God's comfort is permanate. And the more time I spend in His presense the of His Goodness I receive.

My time with God is no better spent. So I dedicate more and more of my time to Him.

David A. Gethes

Dec. 26, 2011

"Not If; But When" Is. 43: 2

   Most people think and believe
that difficulties only happen to
a certain group of people. Foolishly
they believe that they are exempt
from any difficulties. So much so
that they deny and pretend that
everything around them is all good.
   However, the word of God says" Man
born of a woman is of a few days
and full of troubles." God knew that
every man alive would eventually
going through difficulties. And God
wanted to ensure that when we
did, we had the confidence and
assurance that we would come
through and that HE was on our
side.
   God's word says "When we go through
∞ rivers of difficulties, Not if." Trouble

befalls all of us, and there is no way around it. But we must trust that the water will not drown us, the fire will not burn us nor will the flames consume you.

God will not let the difficulties of life overtake us. We are precious to God. We are honored and loved by God. He gave His son as a ransom for us.

Going through difficulties will either cause you to fall on your face or cause you to become strong in the Lord.

Stand still and see the salvation of God. He wants to do a new things in our lives. He wants to show us things that we have never seen before. David A. Mothers

Jan. 11, 2012

Gen. 39:2 "When God is For You...

God is always with His Chosen People. Inspite where we often may find ourselves. Inspite the horrible circumstances that befalls us. Inspite what is going on in our lives, God truly is a very present help and He will never leave us nor forsake us. God will never leave us alone, He will never leave us to fend for ourselves. His guidance is available to us when we seek Him. His Knowledge is available to us when we ask for it. God wants us to prosper. He wants us to do well. God wants us to be the head and not the tail. He wants us to be first and not last. He wants us to be above and not beneath. God wants the very best for us. He wants us ∞

to be victorious. He wants us to be more than conquerors. Success is God's ultimate plan for your life. However, we must want what God wants for us, also. God is very capable of allow us to prosper in all things - family, relationships, business, finances, health even intellectually. The Word of God says "That no good thing will God withhold from them that walk upright before Him". Therefore, we must exhibit an attitude, belief and character that God is looking for and expecting us to have. One in which God is well pleased. God truly is for us. He is faithful and just towards us. *David A. Bethea*

_____

_____

_____

_____

_____

_____

_____

_____

_____

_____

_____

_____

_____

_____

_____

_____

Gen. 39:3" What do others see when they look upon you? No matter who we are people are always looking at us. To see if we are who we say we are, if we live the life that we confess out of our mouths. If we confess to be Children of God, they're looking to see if our attitude, behavior and character lines up with one who is a believer. They're looking to see if we're someone they can trust, follow look up to or rely on. They're looking to see if the anointing and favor of God is upon your life. Those who do not know the True Living God, those who are not believers and who live in a perpetual state of darkness are constantly looking for a way out of their mesery. They're looking for someone to help guide ∞

them out of the hellish life they are living.

Most believers can't help non-believers because although we are very busy, we're not product or fruitful. We have a zeal, but its not according to knowledge of God. They don't show the characteristic of God. As believers, we give God a bad rep. Non believers look at us a see someone who acts like them, behave like them or some one with conduct like them. That shouldn't be the case. They should see some one different. They should see some one who has changed. They should see some one who can help them make the changes their lives desperately need. (David).

_____

_____

_____

_____

_____

_____

_____

_____

_____

_____

_____

_____

_____

_____

_____

_____

_____

_____

May 5, 2012

"Sure Footing" Hab. 3:19

As believers and children of God there will be times when we will experience rough + tough terrains. There will be times when life seem unbearable. The ebbs + flow of life can be overwhelming. Regardless of how well equipped you may feel, some of life's terrains causes us to lose our footing.

We have a strong prayer life, yet our foot still slips. We have a strong fast life yet our foot still slips. We have a strong study life yet our foot still slips. Our relationship with God is strong and faithfull yet our foot still slips. We our prepared best as we can yet life's rough + tough terrain still causes us to slip.

But Habakkuk tells us in 3:19

" That the Lord is our strength!
He makes our steps surefooted like
deer, causes us to be able to
tread/walk upon the rough terrains
of life."

We can't stop people from dying,
lying on us, turning their backs on
us or betraying us. We can't sickness from attacking our body. We
can't stop the foreclosures that
are happening all around us. WE
can't stop the economical crisis
that has overtaken the land.

God's Word says" Their will be famine
in the land but the children of
God will not know it." That's because
God has given us "sure footing". He
will navigate us through the tough
terrains of life. He will instruct us &
teach us the way to go. David A. Betts

June 27, 2012
Lam 3: 37-39, "God is in Control".
The statement that God is in Control is a very strong statement. Yet, how many of us truly believe that. How many of us live our lives knowing and believing that God is in Control.

Lamentations states that God commands all things to happen. The devil can't even attack us without God's permission. Before ever even approaching Job with any kind of trails and tribulations the devil had to go to God first. We are no different. The devil can't attack us without God's permission.

Sickness can't attack you without God's permission. Bankruptcy can't attack you without God's permission. Trouble in your home, on the job, with your children or general can't attack you without God's permission.

God is the filter of our lives. Everything must go through Him first. And whatever He permits to come through is for our good. No weapon formed against us shall prosper. Therefore, we should learn from every situation both good and bad.

Being children of God and heirs of all that God has we should never fret over challenges in our lives. We should never become unsettled because of hardships that we face. We should never lose our peace because of setbacks.

God is truly in control. He, is, the authour and finisher of our fate. It is in Him that we move, live and have our being. Daul a. Beck

_____

_____

_____

_____

_____

_____

_____

_____

_____

_____

_____

_____

_____

_____

_____

_____

_____

Dec 1, 2012

"A Simple Yes or No Will Do"

   When asked a question, how do you respond? Truly, a simple yes or no will do. You are afforded a life changing oppurtunity, yet you are caught up in traditions, protocols and excuses. More importantly, Jesus is trying to change your life, but you are caught up by traditions, protocols and excuses. Jesus want to restore your life completely but He can't get past your excuses, traditions and protocols.

   There is this old saying that goes "If you want what you have never had you must do what you have never done"; and that is rid yourself of all excuse, traditions and protocols.

   When Jesus met the man at the

pool of Bethesda this was the moment of his life. After thirty eight years of battling his infirmity HE is granted an audience with Jesus. Instead of a simple "Yes" he answers with an excuse. What a missed oppurtunity.

What Blessing, opportunities or miracles have you missed out on because of traditions, protocols or excuses? We may have missed out on them once but we don't have to again. When asked a life changing question simply answer yes or no. David A. Gethers

"Being Made Whole" John 5:6

Wellness is something that we really take for granted. We think it's our right to have full activity of our mind body + soul. Truth is, it is not our right, but a gift and blessing from God. For His word says "That, I, desire that you prosperer and be in good health as your soul prosperer."

So what keeps us from being complete whole or well? Simply, some type of disease, infection or ~~Foreign~~ bacteria inside of us. Spiritually speaking that can be jealousy, envy, hate, malice or etc. It could be fear, doubt, worry or a lack of faith. Or it could be arrongance, low self esteem, insecurities or even mental issues. What ever the case may be, we need to rid the body of them in order to be made well and whole. ∞

Like any sickness the best way to get rid of it is by ~~sickness~~ bowel movement or vomitting it out. And once we do that, we begin to start feeling better. So take a close examination of who you are and see what it is that you need to get rid of to be made whole.

Don't be surprised if you find yourself having to get rid of ~~people~~, also. No matter who or what you must get rid of, it truly is worth it. You will feel better and you can go farther in life without that sickness holding you back.

We have been in a sickness state for far too long and the time to be made whole and well is now. Jesus is visiting you with an oppurtunity. ∞ Just say "Yes". David A. Bethea

Made in the USA
Middletown, DE
19 August 2021

45514527R00080